THROW DOWN YOUR WEAPONS

An exploration of vulnerability

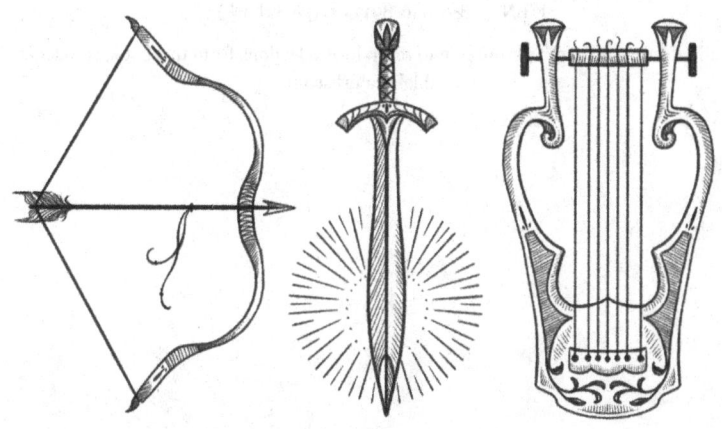

by Blake Cateris

This book is copyright. Apart from any fair dealing for the purposes of study and research, criticism, review, or as otherwise permitted under the Copyright Act, no part may be reproduced by any process without written permission.

Published by Blake Cateris (2024)
Edited by Nicoletta Patsalos

Copyright ©2024 by Blake Cateris

All rights reserved

Cover Artwork by Emily Ann Wells
Typeset by Chip Scanu
Printed and bound in Australia by Ingram Spark
First published April 2024

ISBN: 978-0-646-89175-0 (paperback)

For all information about permission to reproduce selections from this book, contact at:
www.blakecateris.com

Acknowledgements

MONICA STRUT

For helping me overcome imposter syndrome, get these onto the page before I knew I was even going to be making a book out of them and for encouraging me to release them to the public. This collection would not exist without you.

NICOLETTA PATSALOS

Not only a fantastic poet in your own right, but a Spartan and ancient history teacher as well. Triple threat.

Thank you for all the patience and diligence in the world with your exegeses of my ramblings as you combed through drafts, slowly moulding them into the coherent pieces with depth and purpose that they are now—I don't think I've ever seen so much red in a Word Document in my life.

For fanning the embers beneath me in my newfound intrigue for my hellenic roots, I promise I'll stop referring to Greece as South Macedonia.

The now-sung true hero of this collection, it would not be readable without you.

MUM

For being the walking, talking encyclopaedia that you are. Full of facts and a fascination for life.

Also for thinking that one of the pieces that I read to you from this book was Philip Larkin and for giving me your Hopkins and Eliot collections when you learned that I was getting into poetry.

DAD

We like to believe that action means progress, but it's control that's so truly desired. The more we do, the more control it seems we have, but the less we allow for others. If we grip too tightly, we'll find we've crushed what it is we were holding onto.

For never crowding me with attempts to vicariously fulfil accomplishments through me as many parents often mistakenly do, for the quality over quantity approach to your words of wisdom when I flounder and for letting me figure out life on my own terms thank you.

HONOURABLE MENTIONS

Christian Scanu, Stuart Coupe, Andie Pettersen, Katherine Cateris and Eddy Jokovich.

And a further thanks to the any and all that influenced the following words.

INTRODUCTION

by Nicoletta Patsalos

Throw Down Your Weapons is Blake Cateris' writing debut, and will have you craving more from this newcomer. Cateris simply refuses to stop growing, evolving and excelling not only as a musician and writer but also as a modern-philosophical thinker.

His prose is discursive and thought-provoking, but also playful and approachable from all walks of life. His poetry is subtle, expressing a breadth of emotional reflection and understanding of love and art - most would benefit from aspiring towards.

Like all good art, Throw Down Your Weapons is a reflection of, and rumination on, life. It is a collection of pieces about many themes and ideas all at once; among them music, creating, art, growing up, falling-in and out of-love with yourself, the world around you, and other things and people that you hold dear—it's about wants, needs, art and growth.

This collection will take you on an emotional, ethical and philosophical adventure that will either inspire or provoke you into being a better thinker, creator and human.

Embrace the journey.

FORWARD

by Blake Cateris

If you had asked me five years ago, *would you ever write or publish a book*, the response you would have received was *"fuck no, why would I ever do that?"*.

First and foremost because I didn't believe I had anything to say. Secondly even if I did, I didn't think anyone would actually be interested. Third, I wouldn't know where to start. But as in all ilks of the entertainer, there's a certain element of *"Hey Mum, look at me!"* or *"Were you watching me just then Dad?"* that drives all of us to do what we do, so, when it was floated on multiple occasions to make a book of these meanderings, I didn't necessarily shy away from the idea.

What I always manage to do so well, to an unambiguous fault, is find something to do with my time. In this instance it was an experiment of uncomfortable, but necessary introspection. As much as it was liberating and daunting, there was a far more overt sense of thrilling excitement to get into each and every idea coming my way. In the chaos of the great social upheaval at the time, in this moment of our absolution from responsibilities—where the days began to all blend into one, where there was an unspoken, implied permission to just exist and not have to act. It felt dangerous, even reckless to embark on such a mission—but fitting for someone as conflict-adverse as myself. I was well and truly out of my comfort zone. No motivation was needed; it was more-so a deep-seated desire to explore the doldrums of my conscience, dig out whatever may be lurking there and put it on display - and this desire only reinforced my assurance that this was exactly what I was meant to be doing with my time. Rarely am I ever so seamlessly, so naturally compelled to walk out from the shore, out from the harbours and havens that have held me, protected me and stowed me away from harm, to wade through the waves into deeper, darker waters until my feet can barely touch the bottom. This is where exciting things happen.
It was an *exploration of vulnerability* and a bolt of lightening that I absolutely needed to capture.

On the surface, this pertinent opportunity for reflection was my liberation from the social shackles that seemed to fit so tight and comfy around my wrists—a reckoning with my privilege. That simmering away underneath this seemingly-glorious emancipation, was the harsh realisation that I have been living out of balance with myself for far too long—for so long even that all the red flags in my thoughts and behaviour just looked like flags. Through the miracle of hindsight, I realise now that unearthing this behemoth of baggage was a groundbreaking moment, and an instrumental one at that, in making positive steps forward in my overarching goal of self-improvement—which I firmly believe is a journey, not a destination.

It's always darkest before the dawn; as Thomas Fuller would say.

I hope the existence of this book doesn't give off an air of hubristic self-importance. I believe that I'm operating on the same principles as writing and releasing music, which in the 21st century, the means of production and promotion are remarkably affordable and accessible—which many, many other people just like me take advantage of.

These pieces of poetry and prose bound together in this here collection are a mosaic of meanderings that an inherently hyperactive mind had through a perplexing and unprecedented time, locked up with nowhere to go and nothing to do. My aim with them is to stoke the embers of thought that bristle in your brain, to encourage discussion and the exploration of ideas and feelings. They are intentionally non-inflammatory—there is enough blind, conditioned and propagandised hatred in the world, I don't believe there is any need for me to contribute to or perpetuate this. But being encouraged to discuss and listen to ideas you mightn't otherwise encounter is a fantastic opportunity to think critically about the world and your immediate surroundings. After all, questions are the answer to progress. In the event that I do end up causing any kind of unrest, I would love to hear from you as to why and where this happened so that I may correct myself for any future endeavours.

Finally, I hold no delusions in the matter that this mosaic of meanderings may pale in comparison to most writers - actual writers. Not to mention, the enduring brilliance of the plethora of poets, philosophers and academics that have come before me, that currently exist and that will undoubtedly follow. But, as you will come to see in a few situations in this book, I challenge the notion that the quality of art can be quantifiable— those of you who've seen Dead Poets Society, feel free to reminisce over the *rip it out* scene. Excrement. Is it too romantic of an ideal to believe that one person's *The Waste Land* can be another's *amateur poetry of Tiktok?* That just because for one person, through the lens of their unique human experience, one text is unintelligible and the other brings them to tears; that the reverse is not possible for someone else?

As my friend Hayden McGoogan once said *"Not every poet thinks they're a songwriter but every songwriter seems to think they're a poet"* and with this grounding aphorism in mind, I'll say that this is merely the disjecta membra of a singer/songwriter from Sydney, Australia in a moment of clarity and procrastination. Modern & post-modern ideas are explored, the low-hanging fruit of heartbreak & endearment confessed and Socratic philosophical waxing peppered throughout for good measure - I believe that they all have a place in the world and that's here in this book. I'm grateful to anyone, especially you, dear reader, for taking the time to even turn enough pages to reach the end of this Forward. This is my first attempt at writing and, I hope, it won't be my last.

Every word in this book has been written on Eora, Biripi and Bundjalung Country belonging to the First Nations people of Australia.

Blake Cateris
Sydney
January, 2024

CONTENTS

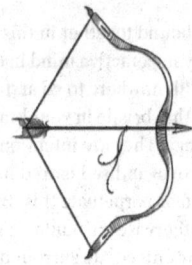

Understanding 1
Entelechy 2
Vellichor 3
Petrichor 4
One Day At A Time 5
Eudaemonia 6
Clandestine 7
Pathfinder 8
Et in Arcadia, Ego 9
The Best Band In Sydney 10
Tik. Tok. 11
Melpomene & Thalia 12
Sturm und Drang 13
Surviving Purely Out Of Spite 14
The Premise 15
This Means War 16
Armed & Famous 17
Gold Fever 18
Don't Leave A Mess 19
Simpler Days 20
Love Yourself 21
Chrysalis 22
The Phoenix 23
Days, Weeks, Months and Years 24

CONTENTS

Throw Down Your Weapons 27
Swimming Lessons 28
Parasocial 29
Despot 30
Perspicacity 31
Tu Fui, Ego Eris 32
Panacea 33
Life Lessons From Sisyphus 34
Quixotry 35
Copyrighting a Revolution 36
Velleity 38
Dead Skin On Trial 39
Same River, Different Water 40
Poète Maudit 41
The Deafening Roar Of Absolute Nothingness 42
Noctambulant 43
Are You Comfy? 44
A Bullet In The Echo Chamber 45
The Pale Taste Of Melancholy 46
The Death Rattle Of Defeat 47
Galère 48
Visions 49
empty. 50
Bleeding Out 51

CONTENTS

Sorrow, wrapped in a bow 53
Novella 54
Amourette 55
Nuance 56
please. 57
The Wanderer 58
Starry, Starry Night 59
Warmth 60
If I Was A Tree 61

The true aspiration of art—
should be to reduce the need for it.
For it to crawl through our capillaries
and imbue our very being
so that we may never feel its absence.

Understanding

Through crassness and compulsion—
we break our own hearts and poison our brains;
we burn through our days and pollute our drains.
Justice is unjust and our wants are a must—
climbing over each other for trophies
that will eventually degrade to dust.
Everything we own is built to dispose;
to landfill, to ocean, to anywhere but where
it could provoke an emotion.

When above our heads the tranquil blue
blankets our minds,
and calms our nerves from time to time.

To be still, bathing in the radiant sun
can wash away the anxiety of missed phone calls;
our debts to society, to friends and to ourselves.

The wind—a current in the undertow,
her direction bound by no man
she's far above our construction.
Gliding like silk through the trees,
whispering to the leaves,
caressing our ears with her
subtle buzzing vibration.

Innocent dependence; a chick's first chirp,
destructive chaos; a hurricane at sea—
there's an elegant understanding
for the nuance of nature;
but not for each other.

And I think that's fair.

Entelechy

To me, a sense of purpose is the most valiant and formidable tool a human can possess. I think that's why so many people cling to the concept of faith; coming to terms with your own insignificance is rough. Those who are first to tear something down usually want it the most, it seems their behaviour merely acts as a coping mechanism.

I see it in friends, I see it in family, I see it 24/7 in my toxic social media feeds. It's a daily battle for myself—and one I often lose. We're so regularly bludgeoned, battered, beaten over the head by the societal book of modesty; and this unhappiness, whether inherent or proximal—is intoxicating and, paradoxically, comforting. Surrender to it once and you will surrender again.

But what if, underneath all this toxicity, this weight, there's a drive—a vivacious passion for your craft, a thirst for more knowledge, a hunger to do better and be better than you were yesterday. A chance to champion self-improvement; to be that person that says *I'm living proof.*

That shit is inspiring.

Vellichor

I went to a bookstore for the first time in a very long time today. A big one too. It was an experience. It was surreal. I usually just order them online one at a time, but the sheer scale of creativity and hard work housed within these walls absolutely floored me. Enticed me. The wealth of knowledge shelved, beckoning the curious mind closer. To physically be in the presence of so much, yet to knowingly understand this is just one minuscule, ageing alley. Tucked away within the vast metropolis of information that the 21st century has access to, just one of these tiny tombs can revolutionise your entire life.

Put your phone down.

Petrichor

The rain is nostalgia
It's chaos and serene
Relentless in its rapture
A madman's dream.

The rain is Mother Nature
Pouring her heart out
Begging us to be more kind
Begging us to press rewind.

The rain is our protector
With a soothing reminder
Greatness can wait.

One Day At A Time

You've lost your voice,
you've lost your crowd–
the air in your lungs
dies cold in your mouth.

Dreams of greatness,
and words profound–
ruined by the faithless
and holier than thou.

The only thing
slowing you down
is the weight on your mind
you carry around.

Take tomorrow
one day at a time
with your head held high
and your feet on the ground.

Eudaemonia

I had coffee with a photographer the other day. Well, we're both fans of each other so it was half catch up, half business. At one point, unbeknownst to herself, she expressed a moment of happiness that gave way to that genuine smile you seldom see on an adult's face. I'm sure you know the one; unerring, unfiltered, unmistakable.

Not the *hey it's been so long, how are you?* or the *I'm in a good mood* smile, it was a rare, uninhibited split second of pure freedom from the anguish of existence. The *I feel so subconsciously comfortable right now that I don't even notice how comfortable I am*, the kind of smile that sneaks through when your guard is down. The kind of smile that would escape even the most hardened and broken down of souls when they are certain no one's watching.

It felt good to see that.

Clandestine

If you're not with me, you're against me.

Through this vessel of opposition, humans have a horrendous habit of building their identity around things they detest. Ironically, shackling themselves to the very thing they're trying to distance themselves from.

We seem blind to the fact that this toxicity stems from our very desire to possess the traits which we detest. Make no mistake, that desire is there - keep looking and you'll find it; clandestine, hidden in plain sight—but only now have you been willing to acknowledge it. Makes you wonder what else is there waiting for you to notice...

This reluctance to accept the existence of nuance is just as easy as it is an abhorrent way to live. From many angles, being quick to jump on any shred of a chance to find common ground with your present company (to avoid ostracism in this manner) is far more detrimental to your wellbeing than the obvious option. We don't drink poison and expect the other person to die, and as adults we don't like unlearning things; it's a blow to the ego. But to refuse? That's equally as counter intuitive as drinking the poison in the first place.

The mere suggestion of changing or improving a habit is of the utmost disrespect because we feel we should have it all together by now. Why? I'm no psychologist but I assume it's because at one point we looked up at our omniscient parents and believed that they had it all planned out and that they would keep us safe. This misconception is one I'm working harder at changing, as I read recently *learn, unlearn, relearn.*

Connecting with people over a love of things, not a hatred.
Fuck I wish I was aware of this sooner.

Pathfinder

I've cruised the lap of luxury
on lands I don't belong
there I lost myself, and my lover,
and the art of song.
I've sown the seeds of selfish needs
and swift they are to rot.
There I dug down until I found,
a reason to move on.

I've channelled hubris, heart and history
through these fingers and this throat,
and travelled the asphalt arteries
of our cities and their coasts;
but I'm yet to find what yearns inside
and I stumble blindly through,
there I burn it down into the ground
and start with fresh renew.

From Sydney Road to Hunter Street
Kingston to FortyFive,
I found that through these heroine's eyes
burns the brightest fire
it's lit a path through the dark,
and the murky mire
as the streets illuminate to snake
round judgement and desire.

But if I stumble once, I'll stumble twice
and likely thrice again,
with doubt and juries beating down
when the road begins to bend.
So I grip the wheel firm until
it straightens up again;
onward north the landscape spills;
the horizon and its edge.

Et in Arcadia, Ego

Et in Arcadia, Ego
Soaked into soil where once was pain
Under the gentle force of rain
And in the ether of the day,
I will remain.

Et in Arcadia, Ego
In the morning birds that sing
In the butterfly's broken wing
In the warmth on your skin
And a whisper on the wind
When there's nothing left to say,
I will remain.

Et in Arcadia, Ego
Etched into cliff and bone,
Each crevice it's own
Canyon calling me back home
And in the shadow of the day,
I will remain.

Et in Arcadia, Ego
A memento reaped and sown
As truth escapes the night
And crawls into the day,
There I remain.

And I will get the final say.

The Best Band In Sydney

The best band in Sydney could have gone far
attracting attention of the scene by and large.
They met up in high school with pawn shop guitars,
a broken down drum kit and a love for their art.

The best band in Sydney could have gone far
with delusions of grandeur and being rockstars.
A hit at the parties but not on the charts
but that didn't phase them; they followed their hearts.

But a few years had passed now, the rifts were to start
caught up in the moment selling out Hiway Bar.
Caught up with the girls, the drugs and the drama,
lost touch with the present, lost sight of their future.

With self-serving ambition, a severe lack of patience,
backstabbing intentions and a cocaine dependence.
They fell out with best friends, promoters and bands,
but falling out with each other, no one had planned.

They think back on all the hard work they've wasted
from goodness and greatness to heartbreak and hatred.
Lamenting on barstools, cynical and jaded,
With no sense of purpose complaining to strangers.

But the mark of a man is not measured in milestones
of malice and misfortune or countless convictions.
So come on you cynics, you sadists and schemers,
who tear people down just because they've succeeded.

Let's be gallant, let's be gracious, let's be mentors and leaders,
let's be every little thing that our younger selves needed.
Because life is no contest, not a race nor a conquest,
let believers believe and march onto their dreams.

Cast off the chain from your leg!
The vice from your head,
you can breathe again.

The best band in Sydney should have gone far,
but they left their city angry, bitter and scarred.
Using people as stepping stones,
they slipped through the cracks;
taking three steps forward and twenty-five back.

Tik. Tok.

Small ideas become commitments,
as the single most valuable
commodity in existence
slips through your fingers.

Melpomene & Thalia

Imagine what absorbing inspiring content,
reading intelligent & dissecting literature,
or immersing yourself in a body of critically acclaimed music—
thirty minutes daily can do for your soul
instead of scrolling, comparing, regressing, resenting;
all in the name of keeping up to date?

Distance yourself from the influencers & models,
the enemies & idiots,
the news & negativity of the 21st century,
arrogance is a mask for ignorance.

Instead follow the artists & innovators,
the thinkers & doers—the lovers & believers.
Dive into their world and bleed from the same beautiful beating heart.
Take a piece of their pain, their purpose or their perspective
and add it to your prism.

Even better; do this without a phone.

Sturm und Drang

Historically, I've dealt better than some
but now, the days all blur into one.
I can't tell my Saturday from Wednesday,
my weekday from midday.
My only point of reference, a recycled routine;
rise, run, rinse, repeat.

On the good days
I have a plan that doesn't go to shit—
which only pertains to half my usual list.
My lonely point of reference, a recycled routine;
rise, run, rinse, repeat.

But there are some things you cannot run from,
or rinse off—some stains seep too deep.
You spend so much time looking at your reflection—
but can you even comprehend
who's looking back in your direction?

Let me ask you this—would you rather
Face yourself while time is on your side
and take life's *sturm und drang* in your stride?
Or leave enlightenment until later;
when time has lost patience?

So rise, but don't run.

Surviving Purely Out Of Spite

We listen to sad songs when we're sad
to make us feel even more sad;
and we listen to happy songs when we're happy
to make us feel even more happy.
When life gives you demons, dance with them.
Show them who's really in control.

The Premise

I took a ride through *Poetry Tiktok* and random hashtags on Instagram recently and thought, my GOD there is some *terrible shit* out there. Then I stopped myself.

These people are using art to process their emotions. They're going through shit and have found a way to productively channel this pain, this love, this amusement to express themselves, and I'm going to criticise them for that? To compare them to my tastes? What I'm going through and my inclinations when it comes to poetry? For a fleeting moment I forgot the entire premise of art and I'm disappointed in myself.

If we get right down to it, art shouldn't exist; but it does because we need it to. We need it to remind us of the beauty, the destruction and all the grey in-between. It shouldn't have to exist, but it does because we are pathetic, selfish, greedy and emotional. We are fallible composites of flesh with ideas, terrible memories and a desperation to exist; we constantly forget what makes us feel alive and what drives us to do the very decrepit things we do.

We need art because we forget how good life can be.

This Means War

A 4WD in the oncoming lane has its high beams and hunting lights on full blast, decked out, ready for war. Even at 2:30pm it's blinding and painful to look at.

This guy is a deadset fuckwit I think to myself.

Then continue straight on for 5 kilometres with my right indicator on...

Armed & Famous

L.A. just seems like a place you move to to weaponise your trauma. A city filled with people living out of balance with themselves, unwilling or blind to the realisation that the answers they seek do not dwell in this pit of indulgence and delusion from which they choose to reside. I can't do that, I'm too rational.
And humble!
But sometimes I wish I wasn't,
life would be a lot more interesting that way.

Gold Fever

I wonder what's so overwhelmingly evocative about books, what's so compelling that they prompt the reader to shout their findings from the rooftops—or in a modern sense, post it on social media.

Unlike a hunter disgracefully posing with their kill or a chad presenting their big catch at sea, the intellectual has not put a bullet into the lung of a mother leading her young to the shore for water. The intellectual has yet to disrupt an ecosystem any further than the pages of this book, which came from a tree planted for this exact purpose.

With clean hands and conscience, the intellectual poses with their trophy for all the world to see, book-in-hand stating *I conquered this, and I am a better person for it.* Perhaps having your heart and mind knocked for six and being shaken to your core by a beautifully articulated sentence, or, entire passage for that matter, can inspire growth, change or even revolution.

Becoming so fully fixated, elated and overwhelmed by your discovery. You absolutely must tell someone about it. Encouraging them down the same path that you took. So that they may feel as you do. To have gold fever.

Literature is an open field, rich with precious knowledge.

Don't Leave A Mess

To be a leader, you have to tread your own path,
but tread lightly; don't leave a mess.

Be honest and be yourself, but not THAT honest;
something more palatable y'know?

And sure, people connect so much better with authenticity;
but only show your highlights.

Smile for the camera and cry on the page;
they want to know your struggle, but not share it.

Knees high, chin up, march proud and follow your dreams.
But remember, don't leave a mess.

Following? Great.

Simpler Days

I long for simpler days,
where my eyes were unglued from my phone
when my mind was unplugged, seamless and coherent.
Those days were ours.

I long for simpler days,
crystal clear vision,
no lenses, no contacts, no blue backlit screens;
just every capillary on those Moreton Bay leaves.
Man, I took that vision for granted.

I long for simpler days,
Summer, twilight, sun,
Family, laughing, fun,
before close friends had since passed on
before things had chance to come undone.

I long for simpler days,
they cramp your heart and joy your brain
thanks to photos in similar frames;
they fill you with the happiest pain
those moments in your simpler days.

I long for simpler days,
when the greatest expectations
weren't the ones I heaped on myself,
when my greatest inspirations
were two gods that could do no wrong.

Before *Live, Laugh, Love*
was an embarrassing cliché.
I long for simpler,
simpler days.

Love Yourself

If you don't know

where you're going,

you might not like

where you

end up.

But you can't know

where you're going

till you know yourself.

And to know yourself,

is to love yourself.

Chrysalis

To surround myself with those that care
Is a helping hand I should sometimes ignore
To surround myself with empaths
Is a blessing to which I should seldom implore
For it pains them to see me struggle,
The struggle is what we live for.

Light may be a symbol of
Comfort, truth and support
And dark may display that of
Danger, destruction and more
The struggle is neither or
But a bridge between barren lands
And green pastures on a distant shore
That reminds us that we should
Take less and give more,
The struggle is what we live for.

The Phoenix

I've come to realise
that I get in my own way
I romanticise and fantasise that
I'm worse off than the other guy.

I yearn for something more
but I burn out in your light,
and when I whisk you away
I keep the pain
and curse up toward the sky.

Our heroes won't stop dying
and our lovers won't stop lying.
Turncoats turn trust to pain
eaten away like rust in the rain.

I want to cry so hard and love so deep,
I want to flourish from my failures
I want to laugh in the face of my defeats;
like a phoenix through the embers.

Days, Weeks, Months and Years

Do you feel landlocked
in your comfort zone,
instead of setting sail
into the unknown?

Throw Down Your Weapons

A long, long time ago—
before the world had shaped me,
I was tough and now I feel cold.
Before the world had aged me,
I was young and now I feel old.
A wave of icy indifference creeps over,
grinding me to a halt.

I look on at the younger—their hunger.
The pride of the hopeful
with fiery dreams—ambition,
their fatuous devotion.
I smile at them because I think I know better;
they should throw down their weapons—
completely surrender.
None of it is any use—
just pay your taxes and shut up.

But then I smile to myself; all this shows me is that
I'm dying a slow death with a full set of lungs,
while the world bursts with life, love and loss
—I lament.
What a way to live!

Or am I already dead?

Swimming Lessons

It is true that we are the author of our days.
We are introduced into the world by well-meaning parents who lay the foundations for our ways; the desire, the passion—flawed by the faults in their architecture and the gaping voids in their logic, we are encouraged vicariously or autonomously to chase our Polaris. The complication is now in full swing.

By the time we are old enough to realise, the gravity of our situation brings us crashing back to Earth. In due course, through the unfamiliar lens of cognisance, we observe an ocean of uncertainty surrounding the sinking ship that our well-meaning caregivers have urbanely ushered us onto. Only while drowning in the debris, crying for help, do we realise how our veneered goals and exacted triumphs have changed almost nothing.

How we are human, how nature does not discriminate and, how we better learn to swim. Fast.

Parasocial

It's a real heartbreaking moment when you discover the source of so much personal growth and self-discovery on the page, turns out to be quite an insufferable bigot off the page.

There's definitely merit in responding to art on your own terms, and enjoying its execution within its own little vignette, separate from its creator. But there is much at stake when separating art from artist and whatever course of action taken—is no easy endeavour.

In suggesting the idea that an understanding of nuance deserves some consideration in discourse, we enter a minefield in which it's far too risky for anyone to wax philosophical *(for fear of the ideas explored being taken out of context and mistaken for dogmatic opinion).*

I don't think power corrupts. They say it does, but I don't agree. Like money, I believe it merely amplifies who you already are as a person, and that corruption has been lying dormant, ever present— waiting to be unleashed.

We are all beautifully, fallibly human and just like the galvanising, chaotic and self-destructive trailblazers we've come to revere—who push the envelope, whose insatiable hunger and burning need for self-expression continually trump their fear of public vitriol; it's remarkable we've made it this far.

Despot

Interesting insights
offer themselves up
in one who cherishes
conquest over connection;
those who'll stop at nothing
once the concrete sets.
In their minds, to belligerently
berate and correct.

Perspicacity

I used to be so tough,
hard on the surface.
I used to think that asserting myself
was a pertinent ingredient in adulthood.

But as I grow into myself, and soften,
I realise how thinly veiled that mask really is.
This is not what control looks like;
this is a lack of.

And I see through these masks so well,
I know exactly who these people are
because I am one of them.

And to look at them
is to look into a mirror.

But my brain is yet to rob my vision
of all the imperfections on display;
and maybe that way it should stay.

Tu Fui, Ego Eris

I'm beginning to fall in love with words; the nuance, the implications, the sheer strength and endurance four simple letters can hold in tying together or ripping apart an entire piece of work.

In music, I can interpret the intention behind individual notes or rhythms played on a record; this comes quite quickly to me—but now the words I read on a page are beginning to make more and more sense in a similar way.

In particular, a phrase which resides in a perpetual grey area of ambivalence for me is; *teenage me would be so proud right now*. Even though I'm guilty of saying it via a veneer of gratitude, *(I think I was merely pretending that my life goals were still wrapped up in the same values I held headstrong as a teenager)* it seems somewhat insulting to the essence of being to deprive ourselves of things we craved in our innocence, whilst simultaneously, detrimental to this same essence to keep our backs turned from broader horizons begging to be explored.

With that being said, I'm sure my fifteen year old self would think I've lost my mind, *"Words? Acoustic guitar? Poetry? You loser!"* And I think some people who've known me since I was fifteen might even say the same.
But that's called *growth*.

All I would have to say to crumple that fifteen year old's world is *"at least I've had more sex than you"* but, the fact that this would destroy him proves my point further; that we are not the same person. Nowhere near it. And why would we be? A fifteen year old is comprehensively incapable of understanding the weight that anyone in the world bears upon their shoulders, how nuanced life is, and how much deeper those nuances are etched with age. But I wouldn't say that to him—a twenty-seven year old should have no interest in crushing a fifteen year old's world. Why would they?

We'd all be a lot happier if we stopped trying to please people that don't understand us.

Panacea

Nothing melts over our minds more mellifluously
than the sound of our own name.
There are no words that drip of sweeter honey
than those of genuine curiosity for the achievements in our own lives;
we love ourselves, obsessed with every facet of our being
and that which our awareness allows.

But giving so much power to the
unknown individual sets a dangerous precedent;
all that positivity can be undone in one fell swoop
from one who has no right to contest our integrity—
no knowledge of our hardships
or milestones in the first place.
That one stranger can rip us to shreds;
make us doubt decades of dedication.

Why do we build our kingdoms up
just to abdicate when the first knight comes knocking?

If you have a solution, I could definitely benefit from it.

Life Lessons From Sisyphus

Sometimes it's easy, sometimes it's hard.

Sometimes you know what's spewing out of you right now is complete shit, but you stay at the table like a bad gambler; because it's been weeks since anything has come out of you at all.

A desperate plea to the gods *(as its mediocrity numbs you over the more you refine it)* the weight bearing down on you that maybe this is the last thing to ever be freed from the traps of your creative confines *(and what's the point of creating something if you can't share it.)*

But now that you've gone over it 10,000 times, it doesn't actually sound that bad.

Thank god you didn't show it to anyone.
... you didn't show it to anyone, did you?

Quixotry

Why do we promise, insist and condition our young to believe that fairytales exist? That nothing goes wrong if you do the right thing and that bad people always get caught. Is this the cause of all our unhappiness and mental catastrophe in adulthood?

What's the alternative? Tell them that good men die like dogs and you should fuck people before they have a chance to fuck you?

One instils hope and the other suggests we're at the mercy of fate.

Copyrighting a Revolution

I can think of nothing more revealing of one's immaturity than to pass unyielding judgement on another work by simply dividing the *good* from the *bad*.

It's far too pointless, misguided and counterproductive to critique art whilst not accepting its greater wholeness, a wholeness which presents opportunity for interpretation and admiration. Alas, this dogmatic doctrinaire has an undoubted intrinsic allure among us mere mortals. Instead, there need only be one overarching rule of objectivity: an objective understanding that a protection of subjectivity is paramount to the enduring emissary within all of us.

In songwriting, there is an ever-changing fluid mix of creativity and discipline, and of freedom and rules—with no concrete ratio between the two ends of the spectrum accepted as gospel. Thus, far too difficult to explain and much too convoluted to teach. And love; simply a feeling, an idea that cannot be captured by the limited confines of an equation or literal definition. There is no way to measure such a personal experience through science, law or reason. Love is a language, but far more infinitesimal in its nuance—and actions? They are our best line of defence against the threat of misinterpretation and misunderstanding.

I guess when flair is fleeting, elusive and endangered, it becomes more of a chance to cherish—to struggle through doubt and uncertainty only to be rewarded with the breakthrough that brings your feeling to fruition or your colour to canvas. Just as hills cannot exist without valleys, night without day nor rose without thorn—to deprive yourself of the negative is to withhold the fullest potential of the positive charge.

I often wonder how certain people can just flick on their creative flow like a light switch— the brilliance involved and required in communicating an idea in a moving way for both creator and audience.

Woe is me; the one that can create on demand!

It's this absence of an objective understanding that has led people to believe that anyone could ever have the right of copy over a chord progression. These progressions are intangible vessels the human consciousness uses to communicate an idea—and if you are lost on the idea that ideas cannot be owned then you are *surely* lost.

To copyright a chord progression is like patenting the use of any kind of wood or metal in the production of a ship—mooring one's soul in the estuary of estrangement as the heart and mind slowly detach. Hindering one's story shackles the creator down to the dock as they struggle to pull together the scraps of a *fully original idea*—does this even exist? Is pastiche a problem? How do you distinguish artistic apathy from a humble homage?

In saying that, is the belief that you were the first person to ever string a Bmin to C to F#min to G in a particular way all the justification you need to financially ruin someone? To stain an entire family name because your greed lines up with that of what a legal system deems acceptable?

It's not a Gmaj7 moving to a Cadd9 that evokes love between two helpless souls, that causes a nation to revolt, that inspires a human being holding themselves together by the strands of their hair to pull themselves back on track. Ideas do this, ideas move mountains, ideas redirect the current of the soul–they are the wind in your sails that spur you on your journey north into the unforgiving sea.

Beliefs are brittle, easily broken–tempers flare and wars are waged, lives are ruined, lost and cultures are wiped from the pages of history because of beliefs–whereas ideas are strong, malleable and enduring. They have the ability to take the notion of nuance in their stride and use it to evolve, to evoke love and acceptance instead of teaching hatred and greed.

To copyright an idea is to let greed tighten its grip around the throat of thought, choking the voice of change.

Velleity

Free spirits get labelled as crazy, untrustworthy, high maintenance, difficult - dare I say, even toxic.

I think this just goes to show that even for all the wokeness, progressiveness, the breaking down of toxic norms, the open-minded and open-heartedness that we profess on a daily basis – it most often just ends up being virtue signalling for social points. There is always comfort in order, in conformity and in familiarity.

Free spirits can't be tamed and you *hate* that.
a) Because you like everything being predictable and nicely labelled
and
b) Because you wish you were strong enough to be what they are.

Most likely you are not free because you are unwilling to put yourself through the discomfort that they are.

It's you that is toxic. The one that is too afraid to take a chance.
Not them.

Dead Skin On Trial

One thing that keeps me up at night, that keeps me questioning and tripping over my own words, is how we value artists in the 21st century. Not as a 'charity case' *support them because they're poor*–but more in the real sense of the word *value*. The pitiful sense of a 'charity case' is due more to the stigma and dichotomy artists have in their struggle of bridging business and art.

We used to turn to artists as our antithesis to politicians; our trusted and honest voices of reason that help us to escape from the depressing reality of corruption in every crevice of our country's leadership. But somewhere along the way, the paradigm of power shifted once more to no longer lay with the artist, but the individual–or more accurately, the collective individual.

Anyone with an audience is now researched and scrutinised, their lives scraped through with a fine-tooth comb by critics, just to make sure they live up to the expected *'perfect human'* oxymoron; we police the very people we rely on to challenge our precedents and social conditioning.

With this in mind, I find it interesting that with age, generations gradually grow weary of the aggressive and ridiculously high standards of behaviour that we set for each other. This expectation of purity forces you to eventually get eaten up by your own principles and it's almost as if, one by one we learn that it's impossible to live life with a clean slate and that, at some point in our lives, every single one of us has fucked up.

By these standards, it's outrageously audacious to believe we have the right to point the finger at anyone in the first place, that now every word anyone has ever said is lined with explosive that can be triggered retrospectively. The culture industry has cultivated a machine churning out generations of artists with no edge and no danger now that all harbour a fear for any expression of autonomy – and I'm no exception.

Art has become boring. A money-making machine manufacturing mediocrity; its value determined by how financially successful it can become instead of how much of an impact it can make on a life or a collective. The rulings that govern the grind of content creation insult the intelligence of its consumers with the dribble it provides them on a daily basis.

By the way, check out my new EP available on all streaming platforms worldwide.

Same River, Different Water

Society is going through a shift in the way it consumes music that is making a lot of us... uncomfortable.

The word *genre* is slowly losing its clout, a lot of us are clutching at our old conditioning, struggling to keep up and always feeling three steps behind. We mock the rat race of the financial world, the CBD sheeple at the top of their steeple but fail to see we're trapped in our own cage; a rat race of relevance. We stay true to old habits defensive in our defence of what we know.

We're threatened by the thought of change, threatened by the notion that what we love will slowly be taken away from us and we'll be forced to assimilate. Hmm... We're stuck inside our boxes, uncomfortable with how the labels we stick on things are slowly losing their relevance - including the labels we've stuck on ourselves.

We defend *our music* with the uneducated, grossly generalised idea that authenticity, creativity and relevance are the only factors in which music is allowed to be judged. That only *our music* can be the sole provider of those traits – (conveniently casting a shadow over corners of mediocrity and contradiction that are evidenced in all shades of the musical spectrum, including *ours*).

We defend *our music* with righteous indignation, as if there are rules to how art can be interpreted and enjoyed; that it can only be deemed a masterpiece if we can understand it—regardless of external sentiment. We defend *our music* due to the myriad of unresolved trauma and confusion we're left to navigate alone, because *our music* is *ours* and any deviation from *our* understanding is a direct threat to our integrity, which must be defended with honour.

Ultimately, *our music* speaks to us without it ever having to justify itself. It listens to us when no one else will. It makes us feel understood in a sea of misunderstanding and that's all anyone has ever really wanted. When the time comes for us to be swept away with the tide of change and lost to the depths of irrelevance, at least we will be there with *our music*.

Poète Maudit

A big reason people are drawn to artists is because they're different. They live, think, and see the world differently to others. They can reshape our perception and existence by sculpting out the perfect personification of love, hurt and thirst. They can cut through even the most well-guarded hearts enabling the strongest of people to break down and cry. It can be the closest thing to therapy besides actually going to therapy - this is why we appreciate them, fall in love with them, sometimes even worship them.

Unfortunately, what most artists want more than anything is to belong. To be a part of what everyone else is a part of; but that's not possible. The only way they can somewhat exist and function on the same plain as society is to assimilate, to make compromise after compromise until they're palatable. And when they become palatable, somehow, they begin to lose what made them so special in the first place.

There's an element of escapism when looking at someone leading a different life to you; what it must be like, who their parents are, what their goals in life are, why are these things so important to them and, how interesting it is that they're driven by a completely different set of virtues and vices to yourself.

When someone seems successful, a narrative pops up *(often sprouted by others that feel threatened by their happiness)* denoting that said successful people must be boring, lead dull existences or be bad in bed *purely* because they shoulder a different set of values to the other. These conversations mostly pop up late on a Friday night, at a table with friends after sinking $200 behind the bar. One person is drunk, down $200 complaining about a stranger's life and the other one is alone, $200 richer and charging forward, not comparing themselves to someone else.

Both with an understanding of what they lack but neither strong enough to make a change.

There's an incredible price to pay for brilliance, one that's much too expensive for most people.

The Deafening Roar Of Absolute Nothingness

Does anyone else feel like they're stuck inside a computer; as if the roles of physical and digital have been reversed?
Our flesh vessels simply serving to perpetuate the ideas which allow us to continue our existence in the ether?
Every minute on the outside is spent thinking about when we can return to the comforting womb of our web.

There's a deafening roar of absolute nothingness; growing, intangible, and thus limitless—sucking up all those in its path. We're entranced and playing hostage to the greatest heist in history, caught up in a global state of Stockholm Syndrome.

Exposure to the horizons of human ability and innovation all at the tap of a screen, followed by the cold snap back to a harsh reality of responsibility and commitment.
I think this is all a bit too much for our delicate human state.
We're not ready for this, we needed more time to evolve.

We shall not overcome, we shall underwhelm.
We're not perfect and that's ok.
After all, that's how this all started in the first place.
Be kind to people out there.

Noctambulant

It'd be difficult to keep up with your own goals, expectations, career and family plans if every time you tried to move forward you realised you were shackled to the ground.

To feel so helpless, so hopeless, so desperate to escape—you begin to question the rules set in place around you. A lack of control you have for your own autonomy begins to bend your biases and suddenly a whole new world of possibilities bursts forth before you to seduce, to overwhelm.

You begin refusing to accept the reality which is presented before you, looking deeper for further signs of inconsistency. Are you woke? Did you somehow stumble upon factual, restricted information? Information with the potential to derail the capitalist structures that play and plague the modern world? Or have you been pushed a little too close to your breaking point, letting your imagination go unchecked for too long, becoming a slave to your own confirmation bias?

The conspiracy theorists cop this argument frequently - but the concept remains relevant when you begin to look past the previously accused, commonly accepted and overt conspiracies. This concept can apply to all ideas that even you, a self-appointed level-headed individual with zero tolerance for bullshit, have taken for granted as gospel without an utterance of uncertainty.

This is the **power** of confirmation bias.

Are You Comfy?

We surround ourselves with yes-men. Our echo chambers are full of them and it feels very comfy in that sanctuary.

You may say *no, my best friend challenges me on my views, we have great discussions*.

No, I say your best friend wouldn't be your best friend if you didn't feel comfortable around them.

How often do you finish these discussions on the same side of the argument? How often do you never resolve the discussion?

You're not being challenged, you're being comfortable.

Try going to work, coming home to your partner and kids or visiting the parents— and in every single social situation in which you participate there are fundamental disagreements on your core beliefs and they're being brought to the forefront of conversation every single hour of the day. That's called being challenged.

But why the hell would anyone want to live like that? Sounds far too exhausting to me. We're way too delicate to survive in such an environment. We need safety, in words, numbers, in ideas.

There are a select few that do live like this but only for a while before they break free and find their crowd, or end up taking their own life. Both options provide respite from the challenge.

I could say one thing to my echo chamber and a majority would agree and therefore I would be right. But I say the same thing to a new audience and they disagree so therefore I'm wrong. But I was right just a second ago so how come I'm now wrong?

It feels pretty good wrapped up, all cosy and safe in your echo chamber, being right all the time.

Truth is a man-made concept and it's a big ole world out there.

A Bullet In The Echo Chamber

It's ok to be grey. It's ok to not know what to say.
In the face of a lover, in the face of the interviewer, *(that just stumped you on a question for a job you so desperately need)* or in the face of that friend *(that believes so much more deeply for conspiracy than you ever will)*. The day is made up of 24 hours, and 24 hours only. You can't possibly have a say on everything; you can't possibly *know* everything.

But it's ok to listen. It's ok to practice talking about uncomfortable topics if you leave your emotions at the door. Unfortunately, no one does this. No one has conversations anymore, no one listens, no one wants to learn, no one has *time*. We just consume, then wait for enough silence to linger so we can cram our borrowed opinion into the vacuum - and there's a sad irony in exercising dominance while simultaneously craving acceptance.

Some days I get angry that the world is left vs. right, black vs. white, Beatles vs. Stones. I get mad that one has to announce one's allegiances to every which cause, every single day—otherwise they are left behind, shunned and branded *part of the problem* by either side of their community. And some days I get even more mad that I willingly adhere to these hivemind, binary attitudes as I death scroll my toxic and absolutist newsfeed. I effectively become a slave to society's algorithm through fear of being subject to the very punishments I witness on a day to day basis.

We are not computers calculating in 1's and 0's.
We shouldn't assign such a backward formula to an equation as complex as ours and ever expect to find a solution.
We are far more than that.

An eye for an eye makes the world blind, and I think that's precisely why we can't see what we've become.

The Pale Taste Of Melancholy

I waste my time chasing my tail
working too hard, not living enough,
that sort of thing.
Too weak to make any lasting change to
the pulse of discontent within,
I even wrote a song about it.

You'd think that would mean I'm
serious about changing but
apparently not. Not sure why.
I've always been a hungry and driven soul
terrible at taking action
remarkably inconsistent at either with no
clarity in how to control it.
Depends how many unfinished tasks
weigh down on me at the present time
I guess.

Picture a child privileged with too many toys,
bored, not playing with any of them.
This is how I feel as an adult.
Spoilt.
A fucking great life, first world country,
parents still together, police smiling at me,
the works.
So many options and things to look forward to,
still I'm suffocated by indifference.

I like singing though,
so perhaps that means I enjoy the
pale taste of melancholy;
that I view suffering as some profound blessing
to celebrate and manipulate into the form of
virtue for flippant personal gain.

But I know that when something is
seriously wrong,
the last thing you want to do is
shout it from the rooftop.

And because of that, maybe
I have nothing to really suffer for
and that's why I find it so hard to act upon.
Either that or I'm lazy.

Both,
probably.

The Death Rattle Of Defeat

What are you running from?
To fill your life with such distractions,
For all your decade of efforts;
To wake and find you're in stasis.

This was once said to me by a wise friend
yet I was sceptical;
Existence thereafter, your name on a marquee,
Your streaming numbers, your death, your self-proclaimed glory;
None of this matters if you're cut off from your community.

How can all my hard work be for nothing?
Was this what the death rattle of defeat sounded like?
Or was this a wise and experienced man practising what he preached;
offering guidance to a visibly lost soul?

Your productivity is a thinly veiled facade for procrastination
And you will die destructive.

Galère

We're all pieces of shit.
No one here is undeserving of criticism.

We steal, we take drugs in bathroom stalls, we lie to our mothers, deny accountability, we turn a blind eye to the inconvenience of one's character—hoping for a beneficial tradeoff.

We're walking, talking contradictions waltzing through life with a white dove in one hand and a bloodied red dagger in the other. We're heroes worshipped whilst we shit our pants, we're gluttonous consumerist pigs—outraged by the fatty, pompous ideas we're spoon fed from the tainted troughs of social media. You can't lie to yourself, no one is exempt from this accusation.

But the truth, right, wrong, religion, your bank statements, equality, justice and science are all just man-made concepts. They are legitimised by the simple fact that we accept them. Legitimised by a majority of simple minds caring about simple things compromising autonomy for sanctuary.
So, if they're actually just ideas, created in the cognisant depths of the miracle that is the human consciousness *(and not rules by which the universe is governed)* then what's the harm in breaking them?

I'm not levitating above the rest of you when I say this; I'm down here in the mud with you. We're all pieces of shit.

Visions

I've had visions
of jumping in front of the 6:09 train.
I've had visions
of punching a friend I made that very day.
I've had visions
of kissing a man that flinches at the word *gay*,
and I know I'm not the only one
that thinks these things but I can't explain.

If I could only spot the tell-tale signs
of shameful hearts and sordid minds,
with guile they hide in plain sight.
True to form and heinous style,
their silver tongues and wicked smiles
breach my walls and eat me alive.

This rehearsal room gets me down
the same four walls, the same old town.
Week in and week out.

I don't feel Zen I just feel blue,
a bitter pill that I chew.
Week in and week out.

empty.

I've never known what you look like,
and though I've spent time in the same rooms as you;
you always leave so quickly
like you can't stand to be around me.

I'm not sure what I'm doing wrong but
I feel like I'm always three steps behind
each time I catch you, I try to hold on
but you dissolve and reappear just outside my reach—
like this is all a game for you.

Maybe my purpose is to drift through my days
settling into a dull existence because
I could never settle with you,
I see faded versions of you in everything I own.
Why do you mock me so?
Does my obsession with you make me any less worthy of your embrace?

My friends say you're good for me
But I don't even know who you are
and I don't think they do either;
But we like to pretend
that you have everything to give
with no interest in a return.

We're all experts in other people's lives,
walking, talking contradictions;
filling as much of ourselves up in them
to help us forget why we're all
so.
empty.

Bleeding Out

I feel wounded.
Like I'm carrying an intangible sickness, rotting me from the inside out.
I clutch my jacket tight to my skin, applying pressure, keeping it at bay, denying most any opportunity to see the bloodied, sticky mess that festers underneath.
They say time heals all wounds but I think I need more of a sentient
helping hand on this one.

I grasp for control of my life, myself and my actions but this only causes me to slip further away from where I want to be. The more I focus on it, the more mistakes I make and the more the seepage begins to stain my skin and brand me as damaged goods.

Most days I feel like I'm being forced into situations I'm not ready for, like a three-legged stool collapsing under the weight of its user.
I feel sorry for anyone around me in the moments I bare with no armour to hide the stains; those who experience the me underneath my jacket.

I want to be ok.
I want to be happy.
I want to make others happy.

But right now, I seem to stress everybody out, choking them with the stench that freely wafts from the internal lacerations I've come to know as synonymous with shame.
As I shed the armour that burdens me with such significant shame, I suffocate all who enter my orbit.

Sorrow, wrapped in a bow

What do you regret?
What do you wish you could forget?
Are you burdened with such a debt?
Well here's someone that I once met:

I find it prophetic that she always knew;
She called it – hard, fast and true
As history repeats and I'm left to rue
Every corner of her curs'ed view

But she exists in a memory,
A memory that keeps crawling back to me
On my good days in great clarity
Of what a piece of shit I used to be

So for this reason I'm glad we met
And grateful to burden this priceless debt
But I bet she wishes she could forget
So tell me, what do you regret?

Novella

A novella–
nuanced, rich and layered
let my tongue flick between your pages
and land on my favourite line,
of my favourite chapter.
Then left to right
and left right after
graze on the grape;
a drop sweet as wine.

Amourette

Sneak away into the night
A little flame brought to light
I'll take you in, here we begin
To deconstruct your fickle life.
We discuss our options for the future
With good intentions, hearts in sutures
When small talk dies, and smiles lie
We give and get so comfort lingers.
"Meet me further down the street"
"Drop me home while they sleep"
Two dinner plates, no second face
I am complicit in your deceit.
Opaque, fake and arduous
A fleeting feeling now frivolous
To give and get, so much less,
Well, this is worse than loneliness.

Nuance

I find a little bit of me
in everyone I see
not whole or halved
but vague and vast
intricate yet infinite
and the possibilities
tear me apart

From the cackled laugh
to the humour dark
hearts laid bare
and secrets shared
be vulnerable with me
show your scars to me

So we venture down
to the depths of their doom
and there I realise
I do not like where I presume

And it's this bittersweet symphony
that stops me ever loving so completely

please.

I think I aged into myself with a grandiose expectation that the word *love* was going to be easy. That a relationship would come by and we'd be so in tune with each other, we'd read each other's minds and say those three words in unison because it felt so right - thanks Disney.

But that feeling never arrived.

Even though it was said to me over and over—I saw it hurt more and more the longer it went unrequited. So, I caved and returned the serve, slapping a brand new band-aid over each gushing wound in the relationship.

The word *love* became confusing for me - hollow and dead in my mouth as the echo of my reticence amplified my insincerity.

The word *love* became poison to me - a means of placation. A way to diffuse someone's desperate demeanour, a last-ditch effort to lift their mood before social situations to avoid the impending ignominy of another spectacle.

I felt uncomfortable saying it to anyone I would be expected to say it to. I wondered if there was something wrong with me but it calmed me to know how easy it was to accept the position of victim and not have to face my fears and fix the problem.

But with you, with you everything has been perfect.
Although I'm scared I'm going to ruin everything if I say it, I'm just as scared I'm going to ruin everything if I don't.

The Wanderer

For all my persistence
In all that seems hopeless
I know not the difference
'tween hindrance and loss

I wander the fringes
Aimless and speechless
Of friendships and bridges
I dare not to cross

The pathless wood
Silently stood
I wonder your secrets
But doubt if I could

This distance is safe
This silence it breaks
Two hearts in pieces
Both misunderstood

Starry, Starry Night

Pepper me with starlight
Take me to the moon,
Lift my body from the night
I'd chase galaxies for you.

Warmth

It was the warmth that got me first.
The warmth of your demeanour,
the warmth of your smile and posture
as you read the menu or entered the room.
The warmth of your openness
as I was open for you
and we received each other;
in a moment of clarity and bravery at last.

You're still warm but something's different—
your flame no longer burns for me
it burns for yourself;
and that makes me happy as hell.

At least you still keep me warm.

If I Was A Tree

If I was a tree, would you want the forest?
If I extend my branch would you cut me off?
Earth-broken, uprooted and logged;
Would you set me free or would I be lost?

I am a tree; but you want the forest.
Weighted and weathered; a life lived off balance.
Where your heart would sing; there is now silence,
a breath of fresh air and a brand new challenge.

I was a tree; but you wanted the forest
I yearn to see you; but if I'm to be honest
If you do not return a mere letter to me
I'm still proud to be just a chapter to thee.

www.ingramcontent.com/pod-product-compliance
Lightning Source LLC
Chambersburg PA
CBHW011151290426
44109CB00025B/2575